Girls Play to Win

LACROSSE

by Bo Smolka

Content Consultant
Chip Rogers
Lacrosse Historian

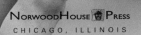

NORWOOD HOUSE PRESS
CHICAGO, ILLINOIS

Norwood House Press
P.O. Box 316598
Chicago, Illinois 60631

For information regarding Norwood House Press, please visit our website at
www.norwoodhousepress.com or call 866-565-2900.

Photo Credits: NCAA Photos/AP Images, cover, 1; Ohio State Athletics, 4; James
Boardman/Bigstock, 6, 10, 12, 16, 34; Red Line Editorial, 14, 46; George Catlin/Library
of Congress, 18; St. Leonards School archive, 20; Aspen Photo/Shutterstock Images,
24; Maryland Athletic Media Relations, 29; Gail Burton/AP Images, 33; Rob Carr/AP
Images, 39, 48, 50, 55; Shizuo Kambayashi/AP Images, 40; Larry French/AP Images,
43; Ben Haslam/Haslam Photography/Shutterstock Images, 52; Clifford Skarstedt/AP
Images, 53; Chitose Suzuki/AP Images, 57; Bo Smolka, 64 (top); Chip Rogers,
64 (bottom)

Editor: Chrös McDougall
Series Design: Christa Schneider
Project Management: Red Line Editorial

Library of Congress Cataloging-in-Publication Data

Smolka, Bo, 1965-
Girls play to win lacrosse / by Bo Smolka.
    p. cm. -- (Girls play to win)
Includes bibliographical references and index.
Summary: "Covers the history, rules, fundamentals, and significant
personalities of the sport of women's lacrosse. Topics include: techniques,
strategies, competitive events, and equipment. Glossary, Additional
Resources, and Index included"--Provided by publisher.
ISBN-13: 978-1-59953-463-3 (library edition : alk. paper)
ISBN-10: 1-59953-463-0 (library edition : alk. paper)
1. Lacrosse for women--Juvenile literature. 2. Lacrosse for
children--Juvenile literature. I. Title.
GV989.15.S66 2011
796.34'7082--dc22
                            2011011050

Manufactured in the United States of America in North Mankato, Minnesota.
198R—032012

Girls Play to Win
LACROSSE

Table of Contents

Words in **bold type** are defined in the glossary.

▲ *Gina Oliver races down the field
with her Ohio State teammates.*

CHAPTER 1

THE FASTEST GAME ON TWO FEET

Gina Oliver admits she was "really bad" when she first started playing lacrosse in middle school. But she never let that stop her. Oliver worked to learn the game. She even made her high school team.

One day, the coach of the Ohio State University lacrosse team happened to see her play. As an African-American player, Oliver already stood out in a sport in which almost all players were white. But she also stood out for her potential. The coach convinced Oliver to attend Ohio State and play for its lacrosse team. Oliver ended up becoming one of the school's best players ever.

In 2005, Oliver tried out for the U.S. national team. She was not selected. She could only watch as the U.S. team won the silver medal at the World Cup. The World Cup is the biggest tournament among national lacrosse teams. Again, Oliver refused to quit. She kept working to get better. She wanted another chance. Oliver tried out for the national team again in 2009. This time, she made the team as a defender.

Oliver and the U.S. team reached the championship game at the World Cup against archrival Australia. That's who had beaten the United States in 2005. Oliver was determined not to let that happen again.

Team USA built an 8–4 lead. But the Australians began coming back. Soon it was 8–5, then 8–6. Australia had all the momentum now. Then they scored another goal. But in the end, the U.S. defense held firm. Team USA won 8–7. Gina Oliver, who was "really bad" when she first started playing lacrosse, was now a world champion.

GETTING STARTED

Lacrosse is known as "the fastest game on two feet." It is easy to see why. Players **cradle** a hard rubber ball and sprint downfield toward their opponent's goal. They might

▲ *Lacrosse is a fast-paced, action-packed game.*

Lacrosse Lingo

check: An attempt to knock the ball loose by using the stick to hit the stick of the player with the ball. The contact must be with the stick, not the player, and must be done in a controlled fashion.

dodge: Any move by a ball handler to avoid a defender. Dodging creates space to set up a pass or a shot.

draw: The play that begins every game and restarts play after every goal. One player from each team stands facing each other with the back of the stick pockets touching. The umpire then places the ball between the pockets and blows the whistle to begin play.

goal circle: A circle area surrounding each goal. No offensive player can step into this area.

ground ball: Marks a change of possession between two teams.

marking: Guarding an opponent within one stick length.

lax: A slang word for lacrosse.

make a quick pass to a teammate, dodge past a defender, or unleash a shot at more than 75 miles per hour (120.7 km/h) toward the goal. Of course, if the goalie makes a save, she might start a **counterattack**. So players have to be ready to turn on a dime, run the other way, and quickly pick up their **mark** on defense.

The objective is simple: Score more goals than your opponent does. And, of course, have fun doing it!

PLAYING THE GAME

Lacrosse has many similarities to team sports such as soccer and ice hockey. It also has one major difference: sticks. Each player carries a stick, or crosse, with a small, netted **pocket** at one end. The pocket is designed to hold a lacrosse ball, which is slightly smaller than a baseball. That means players can pick up, carry, pass, and shoot the lacrosse ball using their stick. Players are not allowed to use their hands or feet to move the ball. Whichever team can work together to score more goals in a game wins. Games are divided into two halves. College games are 60 minutes and high school 50 minutes.

The team that has possession of the ball is on offense. A player can hold onto and move with the ball by cradling it. The player can cradle as long as she wants. She can also move the ball to an open teammate by passing it. Some passes might go 30 yards (27.4 m) or more. The aim is always to send a pass directly into the pocket of a teammate's stick. When a player is open, she can shoot the ball at the goal and try to score.

There are many variations of passing and shooting. The most common, and most powerful, motion is over-hand. To do it, the player begins by holding the lacrosse stick with one hand at the bottom of the **shaft** and the other closer to the pocket. With the bottom hand held away from her body and the pocket by her shoulder, she quickly snaps her top hand forward toward her target

The Men's Game

Some people new to lacrosse figure the women's game is similar to men's lacrosse. But they are very different. Men's lacrosse involves much more hitting and physical play. Men's players wear shoulder and elbow pads and helmets. Contact is hard and frequent. Girls and women continue to get faster and stronger, but the women's game is built on creativity and finesse, not contact. Women's lacrosse much more closely resembles the game Native Americans invented hundreds of years ago.

while pulling her bottom hand back toward her body. The stick acts like a lever, launching the ball out of the pocket and toward the goal.

The team without the ball is on defense. It tries to stop scoring chances by intercepting passes or by checking. Checking is lightly tapping on the ball carrier's stick to try to knock the ball loose. However, a defender cannot hit an opponent with her stick. If she does, she will be called for a foul. Other contact, such as tripping, pushing, or holding an opponent, is also illegal.

If the ball falls to the ground, players from both teams attempt to **scoop** it up. They do that by sliding their pocket under the ball and then picking it up. There is a saying in lacrosse that "ground balls win games." In fact, getting a ground ball is so important that teams keep track of how many each player scoops up. It is important to bend at the

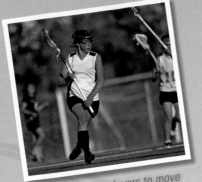

Cradling allows players to move around while keeping the lacrosse ball securely in their stick.

ROCKING
THE CRADLE

No skill in lacrosse is more important than cradling. That is the ability to keep the ball in the stick while running up the field or weaving between defenders. If you hold the stick too stiffly, the ball will probably spill out of the pocket. To cradle, hold the stick— not too tight—with one hand at the bottom of the stick and the other hand about one-third of the distance from the top of the shaft. Using the fingertips and the wrist of the top hand, swing the stick back and forth, so that the pocket moves from about your ear to your nose. As you do this, the top wrist should rotate smoothly.

knees (not the waist) while scooping up a ball. That allows the player to better control the ball as she gains possession of it. Once she does, her team is on offense. She must begin to cradle to protect it from any defenders nearby or to pass to an open teammate, and the play carries on.

THE LINEUP

A lacrosse team fields 11 players plus a goalie. The 11 players include attackers, midfielders, and defenders. The exact breakdown can vary. Some teams play three attackers, five midfielders, and three defenders. Others might have four attackers, three midfielders, and four defenders.

The attackers are the main offensive threats of a team. It is their job to score goals. They quickly change to defense, though, if the opponent has the ball near its own goal. They will try to steal the ball to create another scoring chance.

Midfielders must have **stamina** to run the length of the field several times. They are versatile, talented players who help create scoring chances on offense but also must hustle back and defend their goal.

The main job for defenders is to keep the other team from scoring. They do this by guarding, or marking, the other team's attackers, by intercepting passes, by checking, and by scooping up ground balls.

The goalie's job sounds simple enough: Keep the ball out of the net. But that is not always easy when strong attackers are whizzing a rock-hard ball past your ear, or when a bounce shot skips two feet in front of you. But once a goalie makes a save, she will quickly try to pass

"Home" Game

Women's lacrosse positions are now usually referred to as attack, midfield, and defense. But older players and some coaches still use traditional terms. The attack positions were first home, second home, and third home. The midfielders included the center, left-side and right-side attack or defense wings. The defenders were known as third man, cover point, and point.

▲ Lacrosse goalies like this one wear more protective gear than outfield players.

to a teammate to start the transition from defense to offense.

EQUIPMENT

Women's lacrosse does not require much equipment. Players do not wear padding since contact to the body is not allowed. The only equipment needed is a stick, a mouth guard, and protective eyewear. Protective eyewear became **mandatory** in U.S. lacrosse in 2005. Goalies wear additional padding, though. Among the goalie equipment are a helmet, a chest protector, gloves, padded shorts, and shin guards.

While mouth guards and protective eyewear are relatively new requirements for organized lacrosse, the stick, or crosse, has always been required. After all, you can't play the game without one. Early sticks were made of hickory or other hardwood, with leather strings. Today, most sticks have an aluminum or titanium shaft and a pocket made of nylon. Today's sticks are much lighter and

Playing Hardball

A lacrosse ball is slightly smaller than a baseball and is made of hard, solid rubber. It weighs about 0.3 pounds (0.1 kg) and is about 8 inches (20.3 cm) around.

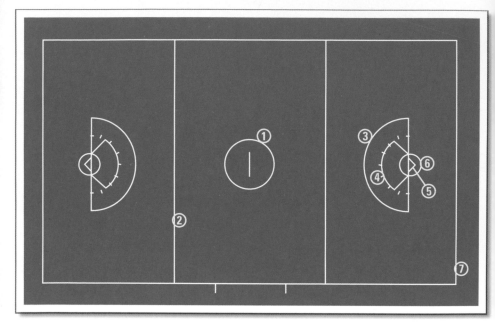

▲ *This drawing of a lacrosse field shows (1) center draw circle, (2) restraining line, (3) 12-meter fan, (4) 8-meter arc, (5) goal, (6) goal circle, (7) end line.*

more durable than early sticks, but otherwise they are very similar. Goalie sticks have a much larger pocket than regular sticks.

THE FIELD

Lacrosse is played outdoors on a field that measures approximately 70 yards (64 m) wide and more than 100 yards (91.4 m) long. The dimensions can vary slightly.

The goals are 6 feet (1.8 m) high and 6 feet wide. They are placed between 90 and 110 yards (82.2 and 100.6 m) apart. Similar to ice hockey, the area behind the goal is in play. That means teams sometimes set up an offensive play from behind the goal.

For years, women's lacrosse had no defined **boundary** lines. It was a free-flowing game in which the umpire simply decided when or if a player had gone out of bounds. Since 2006, though, girls' lacrosse fields have been lined on four sides.

The game always begins at the centerline at midfield. One player from each team lines up here for a center draw to begin the game and after each goal is scored.

Thirty yards (27.4 m) from each goal is a restraining line. Only seven offensive players and eight defensive players can be inside the restraining line. The goalie is usually the eighth defender. If a team has more players than allowed inside the restraining line, a violation is called and the other team gets possession of the ball.

A small circular area surrounding the goal is called the goal circle, or crease. Only the goalie is allowed in this area.

The other dominant lines on a lacrosse field are the 8-meter (8.8-yard) arc and the 12-meter (13.1-yard) fan. They are semicircular areas directly in front of each goal in what is known as the **critical scoring area**. Inside the 8-meter arc, a defensive player must be within one stick length of an offensive player. A defensive team cannot just pack several players in the area to protect its goal.

The restraining line helps create breakaways and other exciting scoring opportunities.

RESTRAINING LINE

The restraining line was added to women's lacrosse in 1998. It was one of the most significant rule changes in years. The restraining line is marked 30 yards (27.4 m) from each goal. Only seven players from each team (not counting the goalie) are allowed inside the restraining line. Before the rule change, every player could go anywhere on the field.

Many coaches did not like it right away. They thought this rule made women's lacrosse more like the men's game. Men's lacrosse has a restraining line at midfield. Others liked it. They said it opened up the game by creating more space in front of the goal. No longer would the front of the goal resemble a huge traffic jam with up to 20 players crammed in the scoring area. It led to more one-on-one matchups and more creative offenses. Young players today have always played with the restraining line, and it appears that it is here to stay.

Major and Minor Fouls

Major fouls are those that lead to dangerous play. They include things such as a check to the head, waving the stick in front of a player's face, charging into a player, and pushing. Slashing is also a major foul. That is when a player swings her stick at an opponent or an opponent's stick in a dangerous way. Minor fouls are for things that might give a player an advantage, such as an empty stick check, guarding a ground ball with a foot or the stick (known as "covering"), touching the ball with hands, and using the hands or body to keep the ball in the stick.

The 8-meter arc is also used for free position shots when a major foul occurs inside the arc. This is an excellent scoring chance. A shooter lines up at the 8-meter arc, with everyone else except the goalie lined up elsewhere on the arc. The shooter now has an unobstructed, one-on-one showdown with the goalie. However, defensive players on either side of the attacker will work to hamper her chances.

If the defense commits a minor foul inside the 12-meter fan, the offense gets an indirect free position. The player who was fouled may not shoot directly at the goal. She must pass to a teammate, who can then shoot.

Lacrosse is a fast-paced and action-packed game. It's time to get on the field and play!

▲ Today's lacrosse has some differences from this depiction of a Native American game from around 1844 in Oklahoma.

CHAPTER 2

THE
EARLY YEARS

The origin of lacrosse can be traced to Native American tribes in the United States and Canada. Tribes in the southeastern United States, in the Great Lakes region, and in upstate New York all had different versions of a game known by some as *baggataway*. In some versions, players held a stick in each hand and threw a soft mass of deerskin. In others, a wooden ball was carried in a stick that was 3 feet (.91 m) long. Sometimes the goals were a mile (1.61 km) or more apart.

The Iroquois, who lived in New York and Ontario, Canada, played a game that most closely resembled lacrosse today. The Iroquois players used one stick, which was triangular at the top. Each team had 12 to 15 players, and the goals were roughly 120 yards (109.7 m) apart.

Primarily men played these early games. The tribes believed the strength and **agility** of lacrosse promoted a healthy spirit. Lacrosse was also viewed as good preparation for hunting and war.

Jean de Brébeuf, a French missionary in Canada, documented the game for the first time in 1636. By the 1800s, French settlers had named the game lacrosse because the stick reminded them of a bishop's crozier, or staff. In 1867, a Canadian dentist named William George Beers wrote the first official set of lacrosse rules. It was on the

Long Games

High school girls play two 25-minute halves in a lacrosse game, and college teams play 30-minute halves. Early lacrosse games played by Native Americans lasted much longer. There was no clock used for those games, and some lasted for several days.

▲ *This team played at St. Leonards School in 1900. With no other schools nearby to play with at that time, all matches were between dorms.*

other side of the Atlantic Ocean, however, that lacrosse was **refined** into the sport that we know today.

"A WONDERFUL GAME"

Women joined the game for good a few years after the men. Louisa Lumsden was the headmistress at St. Leonards School in Scotland in the 1880s. While attending a science conference in Canada, she saw lacrosse for the first time.

In a letter back to England, she wrote, "It is a wonderful game, beautiful and graceful."

Lumsden and her successor as headmistress at St. Leonards, Frances Jane Dove, were instrumental in getting the lacrosse ball rolling for girls. On March 27, 1890, the first-known girls' lacrosse game took place between students at St. Leonards. Students from the school soon were spreading the sport to other parts of Great Britain. Girls' and women's lacrosse had officially begun.

COMING TO AMERICA

Women's lacrosse thrived throughout England, Scotland, and Wales over the next several decades. It is unclear exactly when this organized women's lacrosse spread from Great Britain to the United States. However, women in the United States have played lacrosse in some form since at least the early 1900s. There are even photos of women playing the sport at Bryn Mawr College in Pennsylvania and Wellesley College in Massachusetts at the time. However, the sport began picking up momentum in the United States during the 1920s.

Rosabelle Sinclair had attended St. Leonards and played lacrosse there during the early 1900s. She moved to the United States in 1922. Four years later, she was named the athletic director at the Bryn Mawr School in Baltimore, Maryland. There, she started one of the first official girls' lacrosse programs in the United States. This came only after she had convinced concerned parents that the sport was safe for their daughters.

Over the next few years, lacrosse began to spread to other schools in the East, especially near Baltimore and Philadelphia, Pennsylvania.

At about that time, Constance Applebee was running a camp in the Pocono Mountains in Pennsylvania. She taught the girls there how to play field hockey. One of her instructors at the camp was Joyce Cran Barry, who had been a field hockey and lacrosse star in England. Cran Barry began teaching lacrosse to girls at the camp. The day before she was to return to England, Cran Barry accepted a job coaching field hockey at Wellesley College. She spread lacrosse in New England. Cran Barry also started Cran Barry Equipment Co. That was the first company in the United States specializing in girls' lacrosse equipment.

In 1931, the United States Women's Lacrosse Association (USWLA) was formed at Applebee's camp. Cran Barry became the first president. Two years later, the USWLA held its first national tournament in Greenwich, Connecticut. The National Tournament, as it is known, continues to be held every year.

By the 1950s, women's lacrosse club teams had formed in many big cities in the East. Among them were Philadelphia and Baltimore as well as New York, New York, and Boston, Massachusetts. High schools were getting involved as well. In 1940, just 20 high schools offered girls' lacrosse teams. By 1957, more than 100 did. And by 1978, nearly 250 offered the sport. Lacrosse was on its way.

A Grand Tour

For nearly 100 years, England, Scotland, and Wales were the most active areas for women's lacrosse. England, the largest of those areas, was the powerhouse of the sport for most of that time. That all changed in 1975 when the U.S. Lacrosse Touring Team went to England. Traveling across Great Britain, the U.S. team beat everybody it played. The tour began with a whopping 15–0 win over the England Reserve team. These were not considered England's top players, but the fact that the U.S. team crushed them was shocking. Then on October 8, 1975, the U.S. team beat the All-England Team, 6–5. The U.S. team followed that with a win over the Great Britain team. "From the opening draw, we bowled over the press, bowled over England, and they said, 'Oh my goodness, this team is good,'" said Kathy Heinze, the U.S. coach, years later. By the time the tour ended, the U.S. team had gone 13–0 and established itself as one of the great teams in women's lacrosse history.

▲ *The passage of Title IX gave women, such as these high school lacrosse players, many new opportunities in sports.*

CHAPTER 3

OPPORTUNITY KNOCKS

In 1972, Congress passed a law that came to be known as Title IX. It said that if men were allowed to take part in activities at a school, then women must be given the same opportunities. The law did not specifically mention sports, but Title IX is perhaps the most important thing ever to happen to women's sports in the United States.

Title IX meant that if a school had a men's soccer team, and enough women wanted to have a team, there had to be a women's soccer team, too. The same went for basketball, lacrosse, tennis, and other sports. Over the next few years, sports teams for girls and women began forming all over the country. In 1972, just 31 colleges had women's lacrosse programs. By 1982, 105 did. Girls now had many more opportunities to play sports than their mothers or grandmothers ever did.

In 1982, the National Collegiate Athletic Association (NCAA) took over women's college lacrosse. The USWLA and the Association for Intercollegiate Athletics for Women (AIAW) oversaw women's college lacrosse before that. The NCAA has long been the major governing body for college sports in the United States.

In the first NCAA final, the University of Massachusetts beat Trenton State College, 9–6. Trenton State is now known as the College of New Jersey. The AIAW, which sponsored three divisions for lacrosse, disbanded after the 1982 season.

In 1985, the NCAA split the women's lacrosse championship into two divisions. Division I was for the schools that offered athletic **scholarships** to help athletes pay for college. Division III was for schools that did not offer athletic scholarships. Most of the top players are on teams that play in Division I.

Most college sports also have a Division II. Those schools can offer scholarships but are generally smaller and have a lesser commitment to the sport than Division I schools. Since not many schools offered women's lacrosse early on, schools that normally would have played in Division II instead were invited to play in the Division I tournament. As the sport continued to grow, the NCAA finally added a Division II in 2001.

THE FIRST WOMEN'S LACROSSE POWERS

The first true **dynasty** in women's college lacrosse was the team from Penn State University. The Lady Lions had won the AIAW Division I championship in 1978, 1979, and 1980. Star attacker Candy Finn led the way during the 1979 and 1980 tournaments. She was among the country's elite field hockey players and also led the Penn State field hockey team to a national title. Later, the Lady Lions reached the NCAA Division I championship game every year from 1986 to 1989. They won the title in 1987 and

1989. Attackers Marsha Florio and Tami Worley starred for some of those Penn State teams.

Behind attacker Karen Emas, the University of Delaware had dominated the AIAW's second division. Delaware won the 1981 and 1982 AIAW Division II championships. The school then joined the NCAA Division I in 1983 and won that national championship. Emas had a record 420 career points, with 129 coming in 1983 and 130 coming in 1984. Those were the top two records for points in a season until the University of Maryland's Jen Adams had 136 in 2000 and then 148 in 2001.

Temple University from Pennsylvania also had a strong program. It won the AIAW Division I championship in 1982 and later the 1984 and 1988 NCAA Division I titles. Attacker Gail Cummings led the team to the 1988 title by scoring 94 goals that season. Through 2010, Cummings still held the NCAA Division I record with 289 career goals.

MORE DYNASTIES

The University of Maryland beat Harvard University in overtime in a thrilling 1992 NCAA Division I final. That was a sign of things to come. For most of the 1990s, Maryland was a dynasty. The Maryland Terrapins went undefeated in 1995 and 1996 and won 50 straight games, an NCAA Division I record. Led by coach Cindy Timchal, Maryland won seven straight Division I titles from 1995 to 2001. Attacker Jen Adams starred on four of those teams. The

Streaky

The University of Maryland's 50-game winning streak in the 1990s is the longest in Division I history, but it is not the longest in the state. In fact, it is not even close. That honor goes to Mount Hebron High School in Ellicott City and Loch Raven High School near Baltimore. Mount Hebron's girls' lacrosse team won 103 straight games from 2001 to 2007. That matched a 103-game streak by Loch Raven from 1973 to 1982.

Australian sensation was the national Player of the Year in 1999, 2000, and 2001.

Maryland's run ended when Princeton University from New Jersey dethroned the school in 2002. That was the first of two straight titles for the Princeton Tigers.

While Maryland was dominating Division I, Trenton State was doing the same in Division III.

Trenton State had lost in the very first NCAA Division I title game in 1982. In 1985, the Lions moved to the Division III level and won their first national championship. Their grip on the Division III trophy was at least as strong as Maryland's was in Division I.

Trenton State won six straight Division III championships from 1991 through 1996. During that time, the Lions won 93 games and lost just one. Trenton State won 102

▲ *Australia's Jen Adams starred for the University of Maryland lacrosse team during the late 1990s and early 2000s.*

straight games from 1991 to 1997. In the first 16 seasons of the Division III tournament, Trenton State reached the championship game an incredible 14 times.

It was no surprise when their coach through that whole run, Sharon Pfluger, was inducted into the U.S. Lacrosse Hall of Fame in 2007.

MOVING WEST

It did not make front-page news in 2002, but that year Northwestern University in Illinois decided to restore its women's lacrosse program. Northwestern had a team during the 1980s. However, the school dropped the program in 1992 to save money.

To restart the program, Northwestern hired Kelly Amonte Hiller (known as Kelly Amonte during her playing days) to be its head coach. She had been a star midfielder during Maryland's dynasty in the 1990s. The

Northwestern job posed a tough challenge for Amonte Hiller. Many of the best high school lacrosse players were from the East Coast. Amonte Hiller had to convince those **recruits** to come to a new part of the country and to take a chance on her unproven lacrosse program. That is what she did, though.

Amonte Hiller's first team was made up of mainly freshmen and sophomores from the East. It had a 5–10 record. That got the ball rolling. Two years later, Northwestern went 15–3 and made the NCAA playoffs. It just kept getting better for the Wildcats.

In 2005, in just the program's fourth season under Amonte Hiller, Northwestern went 21–0 and won the Division I national championship. It was the first time any school outside the Eastern time zone had won an NCAA lacrosse title. A new dynasty was born.

Goal-Oriented Family

For Northwestern coach Kelly Amonte Hiller, athletic success runs in the family. As a player at Maryland, Amonte Hiller set a school record with 187 goals. She was a four-time All-American. Her brother, Tony, played in the National Hockey League (NHL) for 15 years. Eight and a half of those seasons were with the Chicago Blackhawks. He scored 416 career goals and was a five-time NHL All-Star.

Led by midfielder Kristen Kjellman, the Wildcats won the title again in 2006. By then, Northwestern had successfully brought the Eastern game to the Midwest. And the team was just getting warmed up. The Wildcats rolled to five straight Division I championships. They went undefeated again in 2009. Kjellman had graduated by that point, but she passed the torch to Australian attacker Hannah Nielsen. She won the Tewaaraton Award as the NCAA's best player in 2008 and 2009. Kjellman had won it in 2006 and 2007. Amonte Hiller's program, which had not even existed seven years earlier, was without question the best in the country.

The Wildcats' goal of a sixth straight title came up one win short in 2010. Northwestern lost to Maryland in the championship game. Amonte Hiller's new team had lost to her old team. But the Wildcats came back to beat Maryland in the 2011 title game. That gave Northwestern six titles in seven years. It also made one thing crystal clear: Lacrosse was not just an Eastern game any more.

▲ *Northwestern's Kristen Kjellman shoots and scores against Virginia during the 2005 NCAA championship game.*

▲ *A high school lacrosse player in Oregon shoots during her game.*

CHAPTER 4

EXPLOSIVE GROWTH

By the time Northwestern University in Illinois had established itself as a women's lacrosse dynasty, the sport was already spreading like a wave across the entire United States. There is no professional women's lacrosse league, but there are plenty of opportunities for girls to play.

Most girls first pick up a lacrosse stick as part of a local recreational league. These leagues are generally geared toward teaching the basics of the sport. Youth players looking for a more competitive setting then move onto youth clubs. The club teams play each other in league and tournament games throughout the summer.

The number of girls playing high school lacrosse more than doubled between 2000 and 2009, to more than 90,000. That made it the fastest growing sport in the country among girls. High school teams play in the spring, before the summer club season starts. High schools that have a lot of players might have a **varsity** team as well as junior varsity and underclassmen teams. The best players are on varsity.

In addition to youth clubs and high school teams, many girls also attend summer lacrosse camps. These camps can be a great opportunity to practice one's skills and meet new friends. Depending on the climate, some lacrosse players also compete in fall or winter lacrosse leagues. In colder areas, the winter games can be held indoors. However, these leagues are generally much less formal than high school and summer club leagues.

With three divisions of college lacrosse, there are more opportunities than ever to play college lacrosse. And in addition to official college teams, students at many colleges have formed their own unofficial club teams. Even after these women leave college, there are opportunities to play for adult leagues. However, NCAA Division I is regarded as the top women's lacrosse competition in the United States.

The best players overall can play for their respective national team in addition to their college or club team. National teams are made up of the best players from a given country regardless of what college or club team they play for. However, since national teams only convene for tournaments or single games, they usually don't interfere with a player's club or college commitments.

NATIONWIDE APPEAL

Girls in Michigan began competing for a high school lacrosse championship in 2005. Minnesota held its first high school tournament two years later. North Carolina and South Carolina also got in on the action around then. In Florida, there were 42 high school girls' lacrosse teams in 2005. By 2009, there were nearly 100.

The pattern has been similar for college teams. The number of women playing NCAA lacrosse grew by more

Attendance Record

A crowd of 9,782 saw Maryland beat Northwestern 13–11 in the 2010 NCAA Division I final. That was the largest crowd ever to see a women's lacrosse game in the United States.

than 2,500 between 2000 and 2010. More than 7,500 young women now suit up for NCAA teams each spring.

Stanford University in California, the University of North Carolina, and the University of Florida are among the top athletic programs in the country. Their sports teams are often nationally ranked and frequently win championships. Those schools all started women's lacrosse programs in the mid-1990s. It is no surprise that they got really good, really fast. North Carolina reached the national semifinals in 1997 in just its second season.

HERE COMES FLORIDA

Florida, which played its first game in 2010, quickly showed it meant business. The Gators built a new lacrosse stadium on a campus where few students knew about the sport. The school poured millions of dollars into its program before it had even played a game!

Coach Amanda O'Leary also had gorgeous year-round weather to promise recruits. To build her team, she knew where to start looking for players.

Of Florida's first class of 24 players, 17 were from Maryland. It was ranked as the number-one recruiting class in the country. That sent shock waves through the college lacrosse world.

"The Maryland-Baltimore area is the **mecca** of women's lacrosse," she said.

Gary Gait

Gary Gait is considered one of the best players in men's lacrosse history. He led Syracuse University in New York to three national titles and was twice named the national Player of the Year. His athleticism, creativity, and scoring ability were unmatched. Since his playing days ended, he has devoted much of his coaching career to the women's game. He was an assistant coach at Maryland from 1994 to 2002. Two of the best women's players ever, Jen Adams and Kelly Amonte Hiller, played under him at Maryland. In 2008, he became the head coach of the women's team at Syracuse.

Referring to her first group of recruits, O'Leary said: "Florida is outside the traditional geographic area where lacrosse is played, so I look at these women as pioneers, trail-blazers, risk-takers. . . . I give them credit for taking a chance and wanting to be a part of something special."

That sounds a bit like Northwestern 10 years earlier. It worked out very well for the Wildcats. The athletes at Florida were aiming to follow in their footsteps.

Yet more and more places have excellent players. College coaches who used to concentrate on Baltimore and Philadelphia now travel the nation looking for their next recruits. The rosters of top college teams now include players from Texas, Illinois, Colorado, and Florida.

▲ *Northwestern lacrosse player Taylor Thornton, who is from Dallas, Texas, cuts in a new direction during a 2010 NCAA tournament game.*

Fans who want to follow the sport have more places to turn to than ever before. In 2011, *Lacrosse Magazine* went out to 300,000 subscribers. Other magazines and websites have formed as well. Television networks such as ESPN and CBS College Sports are televising more lacrosse every year.

The "fastest game on two feet" is on quite a run.

▲ Australia's Lynne Pike (left) chases Team
USA's Kelly Amonte (right) during the 1997
World Cup. The U.S. team beat Australia 3–2.

CHAPTER 5

A GLOBAL GAME

Organized women's lacrosse was born in Scotland
and reached the United States by the 1920s. Lately, it has
spread to virtually every corner of the globe. The sport
has really found a home in Australia. Many top Australian
teenagers come to the United States and play for the top

college teams. Those players have also helped Australia develop one of the top national teams.

Jen Adams is one of the greatest players in the sport's history. She first picked up a stick as an eight-year-old in her hometown, Brighton, South Australia. Adams eventually became a four-year star at the University of Maryland and also starred for her national team. Another Australian, Hannah Nielsen, led Northwestern University's rise to number one in the NCAA.

UNITED STATES–AUSTRALIA RIVALRY

Women's lacrosse has never been played at the Olympic Games. There are major international competitions, though. The Federation of International Lacrosse (FIL) organizes the Under-19 World Championship and the World Cup. Both are held every four years. They pit the top national teams against each other, although only those under 19 years old can play in the Under-19 World Championship.

No Home Cooking

The women's lacrosse World Cup has been held in the United States twice: in 1986 and 2005. Those are the only two times Team USA did not win the title. Australia beat the United States in the championship game both times.

Two countries have proved dominant in international competition. The World Cup is the biggest international competition for women's lacrosse. Since the tournament began in 1982, the United States or Australia has won every title. In fact, in six of the eight World Cup tournaments through 2009, those teams have met in the championship game. Through 2009 Australia has won the title twice to Team USA's six victories.

Friends and Enemies

At the 2009 World Cup, three University of Maryland teammates were suddenly rivals: Caitlyn McFadden played for the United States, Sarah Mollison played for Australia, and Laura Merrifield played for England. Northwestern teammates Hannah Nielsen (Australia) and Kristen Kjellman and Sarah Albrecht (United States) also faced each other at that World Cup. That is a common occurrence as many top players play for U.S. colleges.

The story has been similar in the Under-19 World Championship. The United States won the Under-19 title in 1999, 2003, and 2007. The U.S. team beat Australia in the final each time. The only time the U.S. team did not win the Under-19 crown, in 1995, Australia won. It beat the U.S. team in the championship game. That dominance has led to a fierce rivalry between the two teams.

University of Maryland star Jen Adams, from Australia, cradles the ball and runs away from the Georgetown University players during the 2001 NCAA championship game.

JEN ADAMS

In Australia, young girls pick up lacrosse sticks and hope to be the next Jen Adams. Ask lacrosse experts who the greatest women's lacrosse player ever is, and Adams is at the top of many lists. By the time she was 14, she was already playing for the Australian Under-19 team.

Adams led Maryland to four straight NCAA championships from 1998 to 2001. Creative and unselfish, she could beat an opposing goalie with a behind-the-back shot or make a no-look pass to an open teammate for an easy goal. She finished her college career with 267 goals, 178 assists, and 445 points—an NCAA record. Although there is no elite postcollegiate league for Adams to play in year-round, she has also continued to represent her native country. In the 2005 World Cup, she had four goals and three assists in the championship game to lead Australia over the United States for the title. She led all players at the 2009 World Cup with 26 assists and 47 points.

The United States won the World Cup title in 2009. In the championship game, the U.S. team built an 8–4 lead. Then it had to hold off a late rally by Australia to win, 8–7.

"The best part of this team is that they know for a fact—not believe, know for a fact—that they are the best team in the world," U.S. coach Sue Heether said.

Other rivalries have developed as the sport continues to grow around the world. European neighbors and developing lacrosse nations Germany and the Czech Republic have faced each other frequently in competition. That has led to some exciting games between those teams. Canada beat England in the third-place game at the 2009 World Cup. However, those countries remained a step or two behind the powerhouse Americans and Aussies.

NEW PLAYERS WORLDWIDE

The FIL grew out of the old International Federation of Women's Lacrosse Associations, which formed in 1972. The first members, and the earliest ambassadors of the sport, were Australia, England, Scotland, Wales, and the United States. In 2011, the FIL had 25 full members. Full members are countries that are firmly established in the sport and who have official membership in the FIL. This means that they are eligible to compete in the World Cup.

Today, women's lacrosse is being played on virtually every continent. In Africa, four nations—Ethiopia, South

Africa, Namibia, and Uganda—were identified as "emerging nations" on the FIL's website as of 2011. Emerging nations have been identified by the FIL as countries looking to develop the sport but who do not yet have enough support to be a full member of the FIL.

The game is also gaining a foothold elsewhere. Latvia is a small country in northern Europe, about the size of West Virginia. In the small town of Druva, a few girls saw some men playing lacrosse in 2008. They wanted in on the game. At first, they practiced with the local men's team. Before long, they had enough players for their own practices. Soon, a club team had formed in Riga, Latvia's

The National Tournament

The USWLA National Tournament began in 1933 as a way to showcase top club players. The women who organized that first tournament could not have possibly predicted how it would grow. The tournament, now officially known as the U.S. Lacrosse Women's Division National Tournament, has become an annual celebration of the sport. It is one of the biggest lacrosse events in the country. More than 1,000 players take part every year. Champions are crowned in high school and club divisions. The event also features all-star games, exhibitions by the U.S. national team, and special awards. Recently, the tournament has been held the same weekend and in the same area as the collegiate national championships.

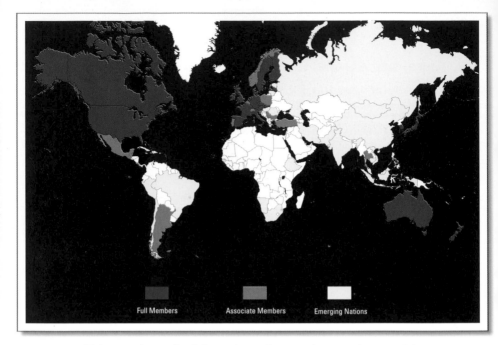

▲ *This map shows the full members, the associate members, and the emerging nations as defined by the FIL.*

capital. Within two years, a team from Latvia had traveled to Sweden for games. Latvia has now become a full-fledged member of the FIL.

"CHAPTER ONE" MOMENT

One of the teams at the 2009 World Cup was South Korea. That team played seven games and lost them all. The Koreans did not even come close to winning. In a field of 16 teams, the team finished 16th. You might think they thought the trip was a disaster. Not at all.

South Korea was accepted as a full FIL member in 2007. That meant it could compete in the 2009 World Cup. It was the nation's first official international competition.

National Pride

You won't find "Haudenosaunee" on any world map, but you will find a team by that name at the FIL World Cup. Haudenosaunee is the native term for the Iroquois Confederacy of Mohawk, Oneida, Onondaga, Cayuga, Seneca, and Tuscarora tribes of Native Americans. The lacrosse world recognizes the Haudenosaunee as a nation. Haudenosaunee players, who live in the northern United States and Canada, have their own passports and, as other national teams do, take great pride in representing their people. The Haudenosaunee women's team finished 11th at the 2009 World Cup.

The team was thrilled just to be on the field, wearing their national uniform and playing the sport that had spread to their corner of Asia.

"We were dreaming of this for two years," South Korean attacker JinA Bae said. "We're actually representing our country even if we're not yet the best players in the world. This is a 'Chapter One' moment in Korean lacrosse history, and we were honored to be a part of it."

Through 2009, Latvia has not yet qualified for the FIL World Cup. Neither has Brazil, Namibia, or Russia. Those countries are all identified as "emerging nations" by the FIL. But considering how lacrosse is growing around the world, perhaps a team from one of those nations will be the next to have its own "Chapter One moment."

▲ Northwestern's Katrina Dowd (left) tries to get past a North Carolina defender during the 2010 NCAA tournament.

CHAPTER 6

PLAYING TO WIN

Jen Adams, Kelly Amonte Hiller, and Gina Oliver dazzled lacrosse fans for years. They could work magic with a lacrosse stick in their hands. Now all three are coaches. They still work with the sport they love, but now the stage is open for a new generation of stars to emerge. Let's take a look at some of the stars who are filling their big shoes.

KATRINA DOWD

Her stick tricks are so unique—behind-the-back shots, through-the-legs shots, no-look passes—that attacker Katrina Dowd is nicknamed "Trix." She won three national titles and scored more than 200 goals in her career at Northwestern. She has since become a member of the U.S. national team. But Dowd is best remembered for one spectacular goal in particular.

Northwestern was trailing the University of Pennsylvania in overtime in the NCAA semifinals in 2009. With time winding down in the first overtime, Dowd took a close-range shot at the goal. It was stopped. The ball popped loose, just to the left of the goal. Dowd dove for the ball. In one quick motion, while in midair, Dowd got the ball into her stick and, without even looking, flicked it over her shoulder and into the goal as time expired. Northwestern went on to win that game and then the NCAA title.

Tewaaraton Award

The Tewaaraton Award has been given out since 2001 to the top collegiate lacrosse player each season. "Tewaaraton" is the Mohawk (a Native American tribe) name for their game that ultimately became lacrosse. Through 2010, only Hannah Nielsen (2008 and 2009) and Kristen Kjellman (2006 and 2007) have won the award more than once.

▲ *Caitlyn McFadden (right) keeps the ball away from Northwestern's Brooke Matthews during the 2010 NCAA championship game.*

CAITLYN MCFADDEN

Midfielder Caitlyn McFadden won the 2010 Tewaaraton Award, which is given to the NCAA's top lacrosse player. The University of Maryland star finished her college career with 149 goals and 110 assists. She led Maryland to the 2010 NCAA Division I title and was named the tournament's Most Outstanding Player. She scored two goals and had an assist in the championship game, and she helped keep Northwestern sharpshooter Dowd from scoring. She and Dowd are on the same team now: Both are members of the U.S. national team. McFadden played for the U.S. team in the 2009 FIL World Cup. She had two assists in the title-winning game against Australia.

KRISTEN KJELLMAN

Kristen Kjellman grew up as a three-sport star in Massachusetts before focusing on lacrosse. It's a good thing she did. The midfielder won the Tewaaraton Award in 2006 and 2007. Before her, no one had ever won college lacrosse's top honor twice. Kjellman led Northwestern to

Give It a Shot

Attackers have all sorts of ways of trying to put the ball past an opposing goalie—overhand, underhand, or even behind the back. The bounce shot can also be effective. An attacker shoots low, trying to bounce the ball a foot or two in front of the goalie. The ball might skip or change direction, giving the goalie little time to react. Northwestern coach Kelly Amonte Hiller has this tip for any shooter: "Players should aim between 6 to 8 inches (15.2 to 20.3 cm) inside the post. If the shot is 4 inches (10.2 cm) off the mark in any direction, for example, it will still be within the frame of the net. Players should pick a specific piece of the net and aim for it."

Many people believe women's lacrosse players should wear helmets like the men.

HEAD GAMES

One hot debate in women's lacrosse these days concerns helmets. Some people think they should be required. Others strongly disagree. They point out that any stick to the head, or anywhere near the head, is a major foul. If girls are wearing helmets, they say, there is likely to be much more contact to the head area. As of 2011, helmets were not being used in women's lacrosse.

the national championship in both of those seasons. She was also named the National Midfielder of the Year three times at Northwestern. By the time she graduated, Kjellman had set a Northwestern record with 250 goals.

Kristen Kjellman was also a member of the U.S. national team and was named to the All-World Team at the 2009 World Cup. She scored 17 goals for the U.S. team in that tournament.

HANNAH NIELSEN

Like Jen Adams, Hannah Nielsen is a spectacular Australian playmaker. She won the Tewaaraton Award in 2008 and 2009 and led Northwestern to four straight national titles. Nielsen, a midfielder, finished her college career with 224 assists, an NCAA Division I record.

▲ Australia's Hannah Nielsen (right) knocks the ball away from Team USA's Colleen Magarity during the 2007 Under-19 World Championship finals.

"If we needed a goal, an assist or just a big pass, she came through every time," Northwestern coach Kelly Amonte Hiller said. "She's just the best."

Nielsen continues to play internationally for Australia. At the 2009 World Cup, she scored 12 goals and had 13 assists. She was named to the **All-World Team** as one of the tournament's best players.

DANIELLE SPENCER

Midfielder Danielle Spencer is easy to spot on the lacrosse field. She is the one who is 6 feet 2 inches (1.9 m) tall, towering over her opponents. But her height is not the only thing that sets Spencer apart. She is one of the top **draw control** specialists in the game.

A center draw is used to start the game and restart play after a goal. By controlling those draws, Spencer quickly sets the tempo for her team. She was an offensive threat at Northwestern, too, scoring at least 59 goals per season three years in a row. She is also a member of the U.S. national team.

Cards

Just as in soccer, the umpire can issue cards to players for various violations. A green card is given for delay of game. A player who commits a rough play or some other misconduct can receive a yellow card. Any player who receives a yellow card must leave the game for three minutes. Two yellow cards in one game result in a player having to leave the game. Any player receiving a red card is immediately ejected. A player can also be shown a straight red card if she commits a particularly hazardous foul such as a dangerous check to the head or a violent slash.

▲ *Northwestern's Danielle Spencer looks to pass during the 2010 NCAA championship game.*

DEVON WILLS

Goalie Devon Wills is brave and tough. You need to be to stand in front of a lacrosse goal while opponents fire shots right at you as hard as they can. That has not fazed Wills. She has become one of the best goalies in the world. She also represents lacrosse's growth.

Wills grew up in Colorado, far from lacrosse's East Coast roots. But at Dartmouth College in New Hampshire, she became an All-American and earned a spot on the U.S. national team. She was terrific at the 2009 World Cup. She made seven saves in the championship game, helping the U.S. team beat Australia. After the game, Wills was named the Player of the Match.

For many years, lacrosse was only known by people in certain areas of the United States and of the world. That's not the case anymore. As more and more girls are picking up sticks, there are more and more opportunities to play this exciting game. There is no better time than now to get out there and start playing!

▲ Dartmouth goalie Devon Wills (center) prepares to defend her goal as Northwestern's Meredith Frank (right) approaches the goal during a 2006 game.

GLOSSARY

agility: The ability to move quickly and easily.

All-World Team: A selection of the best players from a given World Cup.

boundary: A defined line marking the edge of a space, such as a lacrosse field.

counterattack: A quick change from defending mode to attacking mode.

cradle: To carry the ball in the stick's pocket while running. A player can cradle the ball as long as she wants.

critical scoring area: An area at one end of the field where the attacking team is shooting for the goal. It is not marked, but is roughly 15 meters in front of and to the side of the goal, and about 9 meters behind the goal.

draw control: Gaining possession on a draw.

dynasty: A team that is very good over a long period of time.

mandatory: Required.

mark: A player who is guarded defensively by another player.

mecca: A center for an activity, such as lacrosse.

pocket: A mesh basket on the end of a lacrosse stick in which a player carries the ball.

recruits: Players that join a team.

refined: Shaped or developed.

scholarships: Money given to students to help them pay for classes or other college expenses as a reward for skills in specific areas, such as athletics.

scoop: To pick up a ball that is on the ground.

shaft: The long handle on a lacrosse stick.

stamina: The ability to do a lot of physical activity without getting too tired.

varsity: The main team that represents a school. The best players typically play on the varsity team.

FOR MORE INFORMATION

BOOKS

Amonte Hiller, Kelly. *Winning Women's Lacrosse*. Champaign, Illinois: Human Kinetics, 2010.
Northwestern's head coach offers tips and drills for players.

Bruchac, Joseph. *The Warriors*. Plain City, Ohio: Darby Creek Publishing, 2003.
The story of an Iroquois boy and how his deep connection to lacrosse helps him through difficult times.

Swissler, Becky. *Winning Lacrosse for Girls,* 2nd edition. New York: Chelsea House, 2009.
An overview of the sport's history as well as individual strategy and team skills.

Will, Sandra. *Lacrosse For Fun!* Minneapolis, Minnesota: Compass Point Books, 2006.
Basics of both men's and women's lacrosse.

WEBSITES

Federation of International Lacrosse
www.filacrosse.com
The official website for the Federation of International Lacrosse, the governing body for international lacrosse, contains news about the World Cup, Under-19 World Championships, and other major tournaments as well as other information about international lacrosse.

Inside Lacrosse
www.insidelacrosse.com
A source for the latest lacrosse scores and news, covering all levels of the sport.

Lacrosse Magazine
www.laxmagazine.com
The official magazine of U.S. Lacrosse.

U.S. Lacrosse
www.uslacrosse.org
The official website of U.S. Lacrosse, the governing body of the sport in the United States. The most updated official U.S. Lacrosse women's rulebook is available here.

INDEX

PLACES TO VISIT

The Lacrosse Museum and National Hall of Fame

113 W. University Parkway, Baltimore, MD 21210
410-235-6882, ext. 122
Early equipment, photographs, and uniforms are on display.
Fans can also learn about the game's all-time greats in the Hall
of Fame gallery.

Women's Division National Tournament

A two- to three-day festival of all things related to women's
lacrosse. With games involving top teams, clinics,
demonstrations by the U.S. national team and more. The
tournament's site changes each year. For more information, see
http://www.uslacrosse.org/TopNav2Right/Events/2011Womens
DivisionNationalTournament.aspx

ABOUT THE AUTHOR

Bo Smolka is a former sports copyeditor at the
Baltimore Sun and college sports information
director. He won several writing awards from the
College Sports Information Directors of America,
including the National Story of the Year in 1996.
This is his third children's sports book. He lives
in Baltimore, Maryland, with his wife and two
children.

ABOUT THE CONTENT CONSULTANT

A former member of the Women's Division
Board of Governors, Chip Rogers chaired
the National Teams Committee from 1998 to
2009 and authored the first women's lacrosse
statistical manual. He is a prominent historian of
the women's game in the United States, writing
extensively on the early history as well as the
modern era. Rogers compiled and maintains the
national collegiate playing and coaching records.